Anne Martin
The March for Suffrage

FIELDS OF SILVER AND GOLD

Anne Martin
The March for Suffrage

John L. Smith

KEYSTONE
CANYON PRESS

For my grandmothers,
Catherine Curtis and Emma Smith

KEYSTONE
CANYON PRESS

Publisher Alrica Goldstein
Copyeditor Paul Szydelko
Cover Designer Alissa Gates Booth
Cartographer David Stroud
Photo Research/Proofread Caelin De Sa

Keystone Canyon Press
2341 Crestone Drive
Reno, NV 89523
www.keystonecanyon.com

This work benefits greatly from the impeccable research and writing of
historians Anne Bail Howard and Dana R. Bennett, senior analyst in the
Research Division of the Legislative Counsel Bureau and Kathleen F.
Noneman along with everyone who participated in the Nevada Women's
History Project.

Library of Congress Control Number: 2021934110

ISBN 978-1-953055-16-3
EPUB ISBN 978-1-953055-17-0

Manufactured in the United States of America

Contents

Author's Note

Historians prefer to use primary sources (letters, diaries, speeches, and photographs) to learn about historical events. Sometimes facts aren't written down as they happen so historians use secondary sources (things written about a historical event by someone who did not witness the event). With these pieces of information, they have to be critical thinkers that put the facts that they know together to make their best guess at what really happened.

You can be a critical thinker too! Keep reading about history that makes you think and dig deeper. Find new sources and think about how that might fit in with what you already know. Understanding our history helps us understand our world.

Timeline

1912   Anne Martin becomes president of the Nevada Equal Franchise Society. That same year, attorney Bird Wilson writes her pamphlet, *Women Under Nevada Laws.* Thousands of copies of the pamphlet are distributed throughout the state.

1913   The state legislature votes for the second consecutive session for the resolution that allows women to vote.

1914   Led by intrepid Anne Martin, women across the state campaign for suffrage. The vote is successful. Nevada women at last receive the right to vote in local and state elections.

1918   Registered as an independent, Anne Martin runs unsuccessfully for the US Senate. Sadie Hurst of Reno is elected to the state Assembly. Edna Baker of Sparks is elected to the state Board of Regents, which oversees the University of Nevada.

1920   The Nineteenth Amendment to the US Constitution is ratified, giving women the right to vote in all elections.

1966   Helen Herr of Las Vegas becomes the first woman elected to the Nevada State Senate.

1983   Barbara Vucanovich takes her seat in the US House of Representatives as the state's first congresswomen. She would serve until 1997.

2019   Nevada women lawmakers made history by comprising the first female-majority state legislature in the nation's history.

Map of Northern Nevada/California

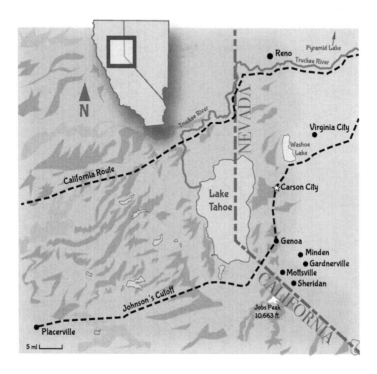

Will I never have any ambition, will I never accomplish anything? O, I must do something.

—Anne Martin, age 18

A Long and Bumpy Road to Equality

Nevada's mining camps even today are often located in isolated places far from established roads. This was especially true in the early 1900s, when the state and federal government had not yet developed the highways we take for granted. At that time, most of the state's population was located in Reno and the surrounding area. In 1910, almost one of every four of Nevada's 82,000 residents lived there. The rest were scattered across a vast expanse in a few smaller towns, on cattle and sheep ranches, and in isolated mining camps of canvas tents and simple stone cabins without indoor plumbing or running water.

So imagine the surprise those hard-rock miners and their families felt when they saw the rising dust that signaled the far-off approach of an automobile on a rutted path worn by horses and wagons. As the canvas-topped automobile came closer, their curiosity turned to astonishment to see that the driver and passengers

Anne's hats gained a reputation among reporters, and many Nevada newspaper articles mentioned her hats.

were all women—an uncommon sight in those days. As the vehicle pulled to a stop, those who could read made out the words on a banner attached to the back of the vehicle: **Votes for Women**.

Intrepid suffragist Anne Martin had arrived to discuss the importance of Nevada giving its female residents the right to vote. Throughout 1914, often accompanied by her friend and fellow suffragist, Mabel Vernon, Anne traveled to Nevada's farthest reaches to campaign for a cause that continued to elude American women: gaining the right to vote. Anne was not the state's first suffragist nor its last, but because of her tenacity and willingness to literally go the extra mile, she would come to personify the struggle for voting rights equality.

Even those skeptical of Anne's presence couldn't argue about her work ethic. She had come a long way, and at substantial effort, to be heard. She found many willing to listen.

Anne would later write to a magazine editor, "This was an object lesson as to the scattered condition of the electorate, and the condition of reaching voters

Anne drove all over Nevada in a car similar to this one.

personally. One would have to travel 100 miles all
day from a county seat to a mountain camp . . . to
reach seventy voters. In one case, a three day trip was
necessary to reach eighty voters."

Voter registration rolls were often unreliable for
those distant outposts. Anne was frustrated, but kept
moving. During one two-week motor journey through
the state, Anne and Mabel traveled to Lovelock, Seven
Troughs, Rochester, Imlay, Winnemucca, Paradise
Valley, National, Battle Mountain, Golconda, Gold
Creek, Tuscarora, Metropolis, Contact, and San
Jacinto. In *The Long Campaign*, a biography of Anne,
historian Anne Bail Howard describes the outposts as
specks on the map, "only three of which by the wildest
stretch of the imagination could be called towns.

Since few of those settlements had any kind of public gathering place except for saloons, they spoke in the street or in a church, local women gathering as much of a crowd as could be found."

In time, the nation would learn of the story of Anne and other dedicated women who traveled to every corner of Nevada's 110,000 square miles to seek support for suffrage in the Silver State. Nevada in those days was a place where men outnumbered women by a wide margin, and according to the US Constitution only men could cast a ballot. The odds were stacked against them.

They were not deterred when their speeches were not taken to heart. They kept coming back, never gave up, and in the end prevailed.

But in 1914 the march toward voting equality continued over rough terrain, and victory was not certain.

Empire City and Beyond

Anne Henrietta Martin was born on September 30, 1875, in Empire City, a smoke-belching mill town on the Carson River in Northern Nevada. The discovery of vast deposits of silver in what became known as the Comstock Lode brought thousands of fortune-seekers and immigrants longing for a better life to Nevada. Empire's noisy stamp mills crushed the Comstock's silver ore, and its saw mills cut pine logs into squared timbers that helped brace the mines and keep them from caving in. Lumber from Empire City helped build some of Nevada's earliest towns. The Carson River bustled with activity from the many boats, rafts, and barges that floated logs to the mills.

In later years Anne described the Empire City of her childhood as "a garden of grass, bordered by cumulus topped cottonwood trees." The "rhythmic roar of the stamp mills" disturbed the peaceful setting.

It was there in Empire City that Anne's caring parents, Louise (Stadtmuller) and William Martin,

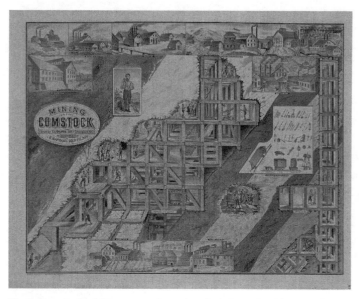

Shafts deep in the hills were used to mine silver from the Comstock Lode.

gained a reputation for hard work, honesty, and a focus on their children's education.

Because there was not an established school for miles, Anne's mother held a private kindergarten for Anne and her siblings. When he wasn't working in his general store, called a mercantile, William served honorably as a lawmaker in the Nevada State Senate. Both parents stressed the importance of education for all their children. In pursuit of work and educational opportunities for their children, William and Louise moved the family to San Francisco in 1880 and, three years later, to Reno, where Anne's education was encouraged and she excelled after enrolling in Bishop Whitaker's School for Girls. It

Anne developed her drawing skills at Bishop Whitaker's School for Girls.

was clear to her parents and teachers that Anne was a gifted student.

One of few schools in the state, Bishop Whitaker was a special place. Young students could learn far more than the fundamentals of English, reading, writing, and arithmetic. As students progressed, they were also exposed to the Latin, French, and German languages, advanced mathematics, art, and music. The school had five pianos for music lessons. Anne was a fair pianist, when she kept up with her lessons, but she excelled at drawing. She excelled at sports and would eventually become Nevada's first female tennis champion. She was also an avid equestrian.

Despite her studies, Anne managed to have plenty of fun and even made a little mischief, occasionally lighting a firecracker to startle a teacher and playing marbles with the boys. As a teenager she found time to play pranks on a friend by slipping neatly wrapped notes to her in class—with a live bug hidden inside!

"The bug and she were both quite lively," Anne wrote in her diary.

Young Anne Martin possessed a love of learning and an independent spirit, qualities not always encouraged in girls of her generation. Anne didn't let that stop her from pursuing her goals and dreams.

At age 16, Anne left Bishop Whitaker School and enrolled at Nevada State University in Reno (later renamed University of Nevada, Reno) at a time when American women still could not vote and lacked equal

As an equestrian, Anne rode horses for fun. Equestrianism also includes horse shows, horse racing, and show jumping for sport.

access to educational and many professional career opportunities. She earned a bachelor's degree in just two years and then transferred to Leland Stanford Junior University, now known simply as Stanford University, in Northern California, where, over the next three years, she added bachelor's and master's degrees in history.

With that, as fully educated as any of her male contemporaries, she returned to Reno in 1897 and helped found the History Department at Nevada State University. She left after four years to study in Europe, but took her hunger for knowledge and independent spirit with her wherever she went.

Anne's biographer Anne Bail Howard has

observed, "As the nineteenth century moved to its close, a new world for women was beginning. She had a part to play in that new world and her beginnings had prepared her well."

"A Task of Peculiar Delicacy"

To better understand the concept of equal voting rights, commonly known as suffrage, it's instructive to return to the earliest years of the American republic. In the Declaration of Independence, Thomas Jefferson made voting sound so simple when he wrote that governments were institutions that received "their just Powers from the Consent of the Governed." In other words, the real power of the government was in the people's hands. They gave their consent by voting.

But which people would be allowed to vote? All the people, or just men? Wealthy and poor alike, or just those who owned land?

James Madison appreciated that dilemma. He wrote that "the right of suffrage is a fundamental Article in Republican Constitutions," but regulating the vote was "a task of peculiar delicacy." If only property owners could vote, then they might easily be able to control those who lacked land. If everyone could vote equally, the masses might be able to influence the rights of those who owned property. In framing the US Constitution in 1787, the Founding Fathers left it up to each state to decide who would be allowed to vote.

That decision left residents of each state free to follow their conscience, but it also led to unfair voting practices. There was often inequality at the ballot box, and a lack of equal representation in government. When the new nation was formed, only New Jersey conferred the right to vote to women. When that state reversed itself in 1807, all women in America found themselves disenfranchised from an essential right in a constitutional republic: the right to vote.

In July 1848, a two-day gathering of mostly women took place at a chapel in Seneca Falls, New York, "to discuss the social, civil, and religious condition and rights of woman." Known as the Seneca Falls Convention, the meeting helped define the decades-long push to achieve the right of suffrage, or voting rights, for women.

After the Civil War (1861–1865), Susan B. Anthony, Elizabeth Cady Stanton, and Lucy Stone emerged as leaders of a growing movement that called for women's voting rights. The women were courageous and outspoken, often appearing before hostile crowds fearful of change and being ridiculed in the newspapers. Their stated beliefs, that women deserved the same rights as men, made them controversial. Still, they persisted.

Artist Adelaide Johnson created this marble monument at the US Capitol shortly after the ratification of the Nineteenth Amendment to celebrate the efforts of famous suffragettes Elizabeth Cady Stanton, Susan B. Anthony, and Lucretia Mott.

Susan B. Anthony reminded doubters that it was "we, the whole people, who formed the Union." At its heart, her argument was simply, "Men, their rights and nothing more; women, their rights and nothing less." But, at that time, those in power vilified simple voting equality as a threat to religion, tradition, the family, and even society itself.

Lucy Stone was noted for saying, "Now all we need is to continue to speak the truth fearlessly, and we shall add to our number those who will turn the scale to the

Lucy Stone (1818-1893) is remembered as a prominent suffragist who wrote her own marriage vows and refused to take her husband's last name.

side of equal and full justice in all things." But turning the scale was a giant undertaking.

The early suffragists suffered many defeats along the way. In 1867, their efforts to win suffrage for women failed to change the New York State Constitution. That same year, their attempts in Kansas fell short. The controversy over who would be able to vote in America continued.

Not everyone associated with the push for equal suffrage agreed on the best way to achieve the goal. Some sought voting rights only for white women; others wanted to include Black women. Still others believed that the cause of equal suffrage went hand in hand with the fight to prohibit the use of alcohol, the abuse of which had a harmful effect on families. In some cases, leaders of the movement failed to find common ground for compromise. But they did not quit.

There were small victories. In 1869, the Wyoming Territory granted women the right to vote and several western states, Nevada included, appeared willing to give the issue a fair hearing. But changing minds a state at a time was a time-consuming process that took uncommon dedication.

When the Fifteenth Amendment to the US Constitution was ratified in 1870, it stated, "The right of citizens of the United States to vote shall not be denied or abridged by the United States or by any state on account of race, color, or previous condition of servitude." But that voting right was only extended to men.

Elizabeth Cady Stanton, sitting, and Susan B. Anthony looking over some papers together.

While adult males were allowed to vote, almost immediately African Americans began to lose their access to the ballot box through trickery, deception, and fraud. Women were deprived of their full voting rights until 1920 with the ratification of the Nineteenth Amendment—144 years after the signing of the Declaration of Independence. Native Americans were forced to wait even longer.

To give a sense of the difficulty of their efforts, consider that Susan B. Anthony, Elizabeth Cady Stanton, and Lucy Stone worked their entire lives to achieve equal voting rights. None lived to see their efforts come to fruition. Stone died in 1893, Stanton in 1902, and Anthony in 1906.

It would be up to other intrepid women, and some men, to finish the journey toward voting equality.

Curtis Hillyer Speaks His Mind

Not all men were opposed to women receiving the right to vote. One of Nevada's earliest advocates for equal voting rights was a man named Curtis Hillyer. As a Union Party member of the Nevada Assembly in 1869, Hillyer spoke up on behalf of women's suffrage. There was much to say, and many minds to change.

When the Nevada Constitution was adopted in 1864, it limited voting rights to "every white male citizen of the United States." That meant no persons of color, certainly no Indians, and no women. In limiting suffrage to white men, Nevada reflected the common politics, attitudes, and prejudices of the era.

It wasn't until 1869, the same year suffrage for women passed in the Wyoming Territory, that the Nevada Legislature considered the issue. Hillyer proposed amending the Nevada Constitution to give women the right to vote.

Changing the state constitution wasn't a simple

matter. The proposed amendment would have to pass votes in the Assembly and the Senate in two consecutive legislative sessions. Only then would it proceed to a vote of the people. If the voters approved it, the amendment's ratification would be complete.

Hillyer's proposal was "decried, disparaged, and ridiculed," as one scholar put it, but the first-term legislator didn't give up. In a dramatic address to the Assembly, he asked his fellow lawmakers to reconsider the resolution and pleaded that they look into their hearts and see the wisdom and the fairness of doing the right thing. He dared those who opposed giving women the right to vote to speak up and state their case. Silence followed.

There were no good reasons, only arguments based on the belief that women were somehow not capable of making intelligent choices or were too delicate to participate in the political process.

"I think we are at liberty to rest until we have heard a statement from some gentleman of his reason why they should not vote," Hillyer said. "The women of our land are human beings. They are, I presume, intelligent human beings. Moreover, sir, they are citizens of the United States. They are subject to every respect of the laws of the United States. Their lives and their fortunes are held and secured under the conditions imposed by those laws."

He called out all political parties for failing in their duty to every citizen. Women could own property, pay taxes, and were compelled to follow the constitution and the laws of the land. But they could not vote. Under the law, even men who could neither read nor write were allowed to vote at a time when a woman, no matter her level of education, could not.

By the time Hillyer finished speaking, he had won some converts among the lawmakers and had probably shamed others. He received round after round of applause. In the end, when the resolution was put to a vote, it passed easily, 25-11 in the Assembly and 12-4 in the Senate.

The fight for equal suffrage for women had passed its first hurdle.

The victory was short-lived.

By 1871, it was almost as if Hillyer's 1869 speech had never happened. Hillyer was no longer in the Assembly. With many new faces at the legislature, the resolution failed. One chronicler of the legislature said, "Whatever became of the signed resolution or who was responsible for 'losing' it, are matters that have never been explained."

The historian's confusion was understandable. The 1871 session appeared promising for those working toward equal voting rights when outspoken California attorney and newspaper publisher Laura De Force Gordon was invited to address the full Assembly. Laura's professional credentials were impressive. She was the first woman to be a daily newspaper publisher in the nation and, after graduating from the University of California's Hastings College of Law, became the state's second female lawyer. Laura was a gifted speaker who had been giving speeches from the time she was a teenager. She was devoted to the cause of equal suffrage and would surely have made a strong and memorable impression had she been allowed to speak. At the last minute, the Assembly took back its invitation to Laura.

With forty of the forty-six members of the Assembly newly elected, the resolution lost by six votes. It was a stunning setback. While the rest of the nation wrestled with the issue of voting rights for women and Black men, in Nevada the fight for equal suffrage was left largely to a small group of unsung and underfunded women who took on the state's most politically powerful players in a battle to change hearts and minds that lasted the next forty-three years.

Proposals meant to accomplish equal voting rights struggled to receive fair hearings in the Nevada Legislature the rest of the nineteenth century as the new state of Wyoming (in 1890), Colorado (in 1893), and Utah (in 1896) approved voting rights for women. Several attempts in Nevada came up short.

The new century would start with the same old lack of equality at the ballot box in the Silver State. But those intrepid women of Nevada were not deterred.

Anne Finds Her Voice

When William O'Hara Martin died in 1901, he
left behind an estate from the family's prosperous
mercantile store that was distributed among his grown
children. Anne Martin greatly admired her father,
a business owner and legislator who had a good
reputation. William had encouraged his daughter
to pursue her education. She respected her father's
opinion and judgment. When it was decided her
brothers would operate the family business, Anne set
out on a new path.

While she was secure at Nevada State University
as the first chairwoman of the History Department,
in 1899 she took a leave of absence from her teaching
position to pursue another passion: her love of painting
and drawing. She studied for a short time at Chase's
Art School in New York City, then she decided to book
a passage on a ship bound for Europe. She studied at
universities in London and Leipzig, Germany.

She could learn a lot from history and from the literature, art, and architecture of Europe, but Anne also knew that she would have to find her own voice. Throughout the decade, she returned to Europe and Japan to travel and write, yet always returning to her home state.

Wherever she went, she discovered women awakening to the cause of equality and the need for voting suffrage. While in London, she wrote short stories and articles on politics and women's voting rights, sometimes signing them as "Anne O'Hara." It was also in London that she became active in England's women's voting rights movement and studied new political ideas, including the democratic socialism espoused by the Fabian Society. The Fabians opposed war, but they supported increased rights for workers and government assistance for the poor. More controversially, they favored public control of privately owned manufacturing.

Anne Martin was willing to stand up for her beliefs, but she also learned that public activism sometimes came at a cost. In January 1910, she was one of 119 people arrested and jailed for protesting outside the British House of Commons. They had come to call for the leader of England's government to support a bill that would give women some voting rights. Anne and others were sentenced to serve a jail sentence in a workhouse for their political activity. Upon learning this, Anne's friend from Stanford, Lou Henry Hoover, requested her husband, the future US president

Herbert Hoover, pay Anne's bail to have her released. But the Women's Social and Political Union (WSPU) leader, Frederick Pethick-Lawrence, had already done so. Anne was set free and immediately left England.

Returning to Nevada, she brought her energy and experience to the already-vibrant efforts of the Nevada chapter of the Equal Franchise Society to amend the state constitution to include voting rights for women. The Equal Franchise Society was created by professor Jeanne Weir of the University of Nevada History Department. With Margaret Stanislawsky as the group's first president in 1911, dozens of women joined the cause of suffrage at a critical time in Nevada history. Anne worked as its press secretary, contacting newspaper reporters and editors and providing them with articles, opinions, and information about the need for fair voting rights. She eventually became the Equal Franchise Society's president.

Change was in the air, but as an educated historian Anne recognized how difficult change could be. Since Nevada's 1864 statehood, many attempts had been made to amend the constitution. Although some efforts had come close, all had ultimately failed.

To amend the constitution, a resolution must pass two votes in consecutive sessions of the legislature, then win approval by the state's voting citizens. Because the legislature met only in odd-numbered years unless a special session was called, the process was time-consuming. That only men could vote didn't improve its chances for success.

Following Curtis Hillyer's impassioned speech in 1869, resolutions fell short until the 1883 session, which saw passage in the Senate but rejection by the Assembly. Both legislative houses passed the voting rights measure in 1885, but it failed in 1887.

Some strides were made. Long before they were allowed to serve as lawmakers, beginning in 1875 women started to appear at the legislature as lobbyists, reporters, copyists, secretaries, and public speakers. In an era before typewriters were common, many of the women were valued for their superior penmanship. By the end of the century approximately half of all staffers would be female. Historian Dana Bennett observes, "Their active and abundant presence demonstrated that the process was not entirely male and that many women, with diverse agendas, moved with confidence through this environment."

The 1887 session saw a separate resolution pass that would amend the constitution to enable women to be elected to school superintendent and trustee positions—they just couldn't vote for themselves. When the resolution became law in 1890, eight women won elections across the state. By the end of the century, women's faces would become commonplace on school boards in Nevada.

They still lacked the right to vote.

Momentum was building though. Nevada women started their own suffrage newspaper, and the size of their clubs and organizations swelled to hundreds of members. Some elected officials saw the inevitable change coming and supported it. Perhaps they believed in the cause or were afraid of being on the wrong side of history. Others remained opposed.

Just as women were gaining real power to influence the public school system, the legislature changed the law and they were again prevented from running for the leadership position of school superintendent. It was a temporary step backward. The 1909 legislature passed a joint resolution to return the rights of women to serve in superintendent positions. The struggle continued.

The cause of suffrage benefited greatly from the efforts of attorney Felice Cohn. Born in 1878 in Carson City, she was small in stature, but mighty in intellect and represented a different side of Nevada's suffrage movement. Unlike Anne, who was an outspoken voice for change, Felice was most effective lobbying government from the inside. She worked the halls of power in the legislature and was respected for her measured approach.

Building consensus at the legislature, Felice drafted the proposed change to the constitution, which read, "There should be no denial of the elective franchise at any election on account of sex."

Anne and Felice differed greatly on the best path toward success. Anne was louder. Some of her critics considered her too aggressive and combative. They said she used language that made her seem prone to violence. In reality, Anne was a peace activist.

Remember that by the early 1900s the push toward equal voting rights was more than sixty years old. Different suffrage groups used varying strategies. Some chose to challenge male-only voting laws, others took to the streets in parades and protests. Some chose silent candlelight vigils. Still others went on hunger strikes.

Felice was sometimes criticized for being too close to the state's politically powerful. But as Jean Ford and Kay Sanders wrote, "It is important to note that we are not talking guns and aggression here; we are talking about pushing for a Federal amendment with parades and demonstrations."

Although Felice was a founding member of the Nevada Equal Franchise Society and was rightly credited with persuading lawmakers to vote to pass a constitutional resolution in 1911, she eventually separated from the group. Felice later started the Non-Militant Equal Suffrage Society and the Nevada Voter's Club, organizations that brought together women to participate in the election process.

It's fair to say that Anne and Felice each were effective in their own way. Both were well known in Washington, DC, and respected by Nevada elected officials. Both influenced hundreds of women, and like-minded men, on the subject of equal suffrage at the state and national levels.

Anne found an ally in Bird May Wilson, vice president of the Equal Franchise Society and the seventh licensed female attorney in Nevada. Like

SUFFRAGE

AND

GOVERNMENT

The Modern Idea of Government by Consent and Woman's
Place in it, with special reference to Nevada
and other Western States

By

MARY AUSTIN , *1868-1934*
Author of "A Woman of Genius", Etc. Etc.

and

ANNE MARTIN
President of Nevada Equal Franchise Society

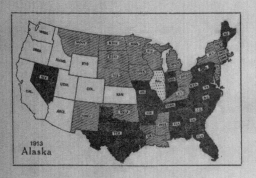

1913
Alaska

Published for the
NEVADA EQUAL FRANCHISE SOCIETY
153 North Virginia Street, Reno, Nevada
by the
NATIONAL AMERICAN WOMAN SUFFRAGE ASSOCIATION
505 Fifth Avenue   New York City
1914

Suffrage and Government was one of many books, essays, articles, pamphlets, and stories that Anne wrote to spread the word about women's suffrage.

George Wingfield fought to keep gambling scenes, like this Reno casino in 1910, open for business.

Felice, Bird had been immersed in the law throughout her life, rising from secretary to appeals court clerk and eventually becoming a licensed lawyer. And like Felice, Bird was an effective lobbyist at the legislature.

The cause of suffrage would need all the help it could get. Powerful banker, gambling, and mining boss George Wingfield, known as the "King of Nevada" because of his influence over elected officials, opposed suffrage. George and others believed that if women won their right to vote they might move to outlaw liquor sales and consumption or close the gambling dens that existed openly despite the fact that they were illegal. In short, women with the right to vote might be bad for business.

US Senator Francis Newlands and Governor Tasker Oddie, who were popular and influenced many of the

Not all men were against women's suffrage. Some, like these from the Men's Suffrage League in New York, believed strongly in a woman's right to vote.

state's voters, quietly supported woman's suffrage. But that was no guarantee of success. Bird, who practiced law and understood George's power, was not intimidated.

A persuasive speaker and even better writer, in 1913 she penned a slender pamphlet *Women Under Nevada Laws* that criticized the lack of fairness and equality experienced by women in the state. The pamphlet outlined bias in Nevada statutes and argued that the laws should be written to ensure that men and women receive equal treatment.

Twenty thousand copies of her pamphlet were printed and distributed throughout the state by the Equal Franchise Society. Many read Bird Wilson's pamphlet. Her efforts were substantially responsible for educating women about how the law actually worked against them. For instance, women who owned land had to pay property taxes, but they could not vote. A married woman who worked and earned money didn't control their earnings. Her husband did.

"And although Nevada is more liberal in its treatment of women than many states," Bird wrote, "there is still unjust discrimination between the rights of women and the rights of men, and this will never be remedied until the women themselves have the power to make laws."

That meant winning the right to vote. It also meant focusing, often for the first time, on social reforms such as the prohibition of alcoholic beverages that strived to improve the lives of families.

"The movement has been carried almost through," Bird wrote. "The last pull must be the strongest, that the voters may know it is not only an inherent right, but the wish of the people of Nevada that her women should be given the justice and dignity of enfranchisement."

George Wingfield was on his way to a rare loss before the legislature. Seeing the tide turn against him, he proclaimed that he would leave the state if the suffrage issue were successful. It passed both houses of the legislature in 1913. George stayed in Nevada—and watched history happen before his disbelieving eyes.

The Roughest Road to Success

With the legislative victories secured at last, now all those seeking voting rights for women had to do was persuade enough male voters to support their cause. With George Wingfield influencing business owners in the population centers of Reno, Carson City, and Virginia City, Anne Martin and her allies took to the rocky road to victory across the vast Nevada outback. There were plenty of votes to win—if you could reach them.

Loading up their roadster, Anne and her compatriots, often accompanied by fellow suffragist Mabel Vernon, took out to the distant parts of the state. They reached out to every county, community, and sparsely populated mining camp, cattle ranch, and sheep camp.

They weren't always warmly received, and sometimes they were ignored, but they never stopped campaigning and never gave up. Anne often called Nevada the "most male" state in the Union. She also called on her national contacts in the women's suffrage movement to speak out on equal voting rights from Reno to Las Vegas. She worked tirelessly, giving speeches, writing newspaper stories, and traveling, always traveling, to the farthest reaches of the state. Meanwhile, Bird Wilson campaigned energetically from Goldfield to Las Vegas.

Not just men, but some women also were against equal voting rights. One was Emma Adams, wife of former Nevada governor Jewett Adams, who served as president of the Nevada Association of Women Opposed to Equal Suffrage.

Not just women, but some men also supported voting rights for all. The year 1914 saw the rise of the Nevada Men's Suffrage League, which vocally supported equal voting rights. James Gault, a state senator from Washoe County in the north, was an outspoken suffragist. In 1914 Gault wrote forcefully, "Vote for the women at the coming election. We will have better government. They are this dark world's light. If it was not for the women, this world would go back into darkness where it was six thousand years ago."

In the end, Nevada's male registered voters went to the polls November 3, 1914. Although George Wingfield's influence held sway in Reno, Carson City, and Virginia City, Anne's efforts across the state paid off. The final tally: 10,936 in favor, 7,258 in opposition. The state's equal suffrage amendment had passed!

For the first time, Nevada women would be able to vote in local and state elections. But they still couldn't

Nevada Governor Emmet D. Boyle signs the resolution for notification of Nineteenth Amendment to Constitution of the US.

vote in federal races for members of Congress and the president. For that, an amendment to the US Constitution would be necessary.

No one had to remind Anne and her allies that change took time and great effort. They immediately went back to work.

Anne's success as a suffrage leader in Nevada made national headlines and greatly increased her profile. She continued to organize women's groups in the West and traveled often to Washington, DC, to speak and participate as a ranking member of the National American Woman Suffrage Association, Congressional

Union, and National Woman's Party (NWP.) She understood well that women, with the right to vote, would represent a new and powerful force in American politics. She became more outspoken than ever.

But it was as a member of the NWP's Silent Sentinels, women who routinely, quietly protested outside the White House, that on July 14, 1917, Anne and others were arrested. It meant another sentence for disturbing the peace, another trip to a workhouse, but the news proved to be an embarrassment to President Woodrow Wilson, a Democrat who had been slow to embrace the great change coming to American society. Anne, so often Wilson's critic, was pardoned by the president after a few days in detention.

The incarceration failed to dampen Anne's spirits, but the arrest was used in the press to label her as a person who was outside the mainstream, even militant.

She returned to Nevada eager to make change from the inside of government. She determined that the best way to do that was to run for public office.

GAT — Get Anne There!

When Francis Newlands, Nevada's powerful US senator, died of heart failure on Christmas Eve 1917, Governor Emmet Boyle appointed longtime public servant Charles Henderson to replace him. Henderson was a well-known member of the Democratic Party and had served in the state Assembly and as a University Regent, but he was just another freshman senator when he took office in January 1918. Although he had the equivalent of a head start, he would still have to run in a special election in November.

That gave Anne Martin an idea that must have seemed outrageous. She would become the first woman in American history to run for the US Senate!

She was well acquainted with Washington, DC, and well known in its political circles as an articulate, outspoken suffragist and political progressive who supported government programs that helped the poor and uplifted women. With high name recognition from her years on the suffrage campaign, Anne decided to enter politics at the highest level. Although some of her friends attempted to persuade her to try for an office closer to home, she was determined to run for the Senate. It was a bold move.

Anne's decision was influenced by the 1916 election in Montana of Jeannette Rankin, a suffragist and political progressive who became the first female member of the US House of Representatives. "I am deeply conscious of the responsibility resting upon me," Jeannette said in her victory statement. "I may be the first woman member of Congress. But I won't be the last."

Like Jeannette, Anne was a progressive who focused her campaign on improving workers' rights, fixing the ills of society, improving basic education, and remaining out of the war that was raging across Europe.

Her many years working on behalf of women's suffrage gave her valuable experience when she entered the race independent of either major party, but even her closest friends knew she was a substantial underdog. Not only had no woman ever run for the Senate, but she also found herself running against Nevada's powerful business and banking interests.

Many residents who had supported her in the fight for women's voting rights found themselves disagreeing with Anne's positions on other issues such as prohibition. It was fine that she said she wanted to serve as a positive influence for women in political life, but when she called for turning over the privately

Prohibition was only partially successful because lots of people still tried to sneak alcoholic drinks through the country. Prohibition agents would poor the alcohol they found down into the sewers.

owned railroads and utilities to government control, she lost support. That was simply too much change for many voters to imagine, even at a time when other nations were experimenting with their political and economic systems.

Anne's entry into the Senate campaign raised its profile considerably, drawing reporters from as far away as New York City to cover the race and interview the ambitious woman. To some, she was a curiosity. To others, she represented a threat to the traditional role of women as homemakers. Still others believed that her presence on the campaign trail was a sign of progress for women—even if she was not the favorite to win.

The uniqueness of her candidacy made her a curiosity to national journalists, who generally treated Anne's candidacy with respect and were even favorable to her positions on issues. Most Nevada reporters, on the other hand, were critical of the idea of a woman running for such a prestigious office. Getting the right to vote was one thing, being in charge of the decision-making was quite another.

Some Nevada newspaper writers were openly hostile toward her. Although she had advanced university degrees in history, they questioned her intelligence and knowledge of history. They dismissed her progressive politics, and some considered her a radical. They scoffed at her speeches and belittled her at every turn. They even made fun of the way she dressed, taking special delight in criticizing her hat. When she discussed political ideas being tested in other countries, they questioned her love of America.

She was not intimidated. Her biographer writes, "When the press laughed and taunted, she endured and did not cry foul." Instead, she just worked harder.

"I am pledged to no party," she said, "but to the interests of the whole people."

She also pledged to be fair—to all the people.

"It is fairness not just to myself, nor just to women, but fairness to the state and to the nation," she said. "Patriotism demands that our country have the full benefit of woman's experience."

The miners of the towns Anne traveled to often worked in shafts like this one from Bullfrog Mine in Nye County, Nevada.

Her campaign slogan during her run for Senate was "GAT—Get Anne There."

Organizers went to saloons, as Anne's campaign manager wrote, "danced with cowboys in country schoolhouses, dropped down mine shafts and climbed up reefs in search of the elusive vote. They have broken down on the open desert, only the alkali in sight, when motoring with their canteens and their lunch box. They have slept out in their blankets in the lee of a sage brush and listened to the howling of the coyotes."

Anne worked relentlessly, traveling around the state many times and making as many as five speeches a day even when journalists and other critics tried to laugh off her campaign efforts. Her male opponents, they noted, barely campaigned at all.

The November 5 election wasn't close. An exhausted Anne placed third behind the winner, Henderson, and the runner-up, E. E. Roberts, whose newspaper had been cruel to Anne. When all the ballots were tallied, she finished with 4,603 votes—far behind Henderson's 12,197 and the 8,053 Roberts collected.

She tried to balance her devotion to the cause of equal suffrage with her own personal political interests and desires to be seen as a national leader. She had many followers, but she also made some enemies in the movement toward achieving greater justice for women.

In striving to be heard, she didn't always listen.

But even in defeat she saw the greater lesson of her candidacy, observing that "even if I should not win, it will never seem so strange when a woman tries it."

Her biographer reminds us of Anne's remarkable success against long odds, the press, and "the very country against her. That she did not quit public life altogether is surprising."

Anne's tenacity and dedication to her cause also won the respect of the *Oakland Tribune* newspaper, which noted that she had captured the attention "of men and women who had never before given the woman's viewpoint much thought.

"So if Anne didn't win, she didn't lose. Her campaign talks were little classics, in the sense that she talked of real things and real issues, shorn of the 'bunk' of most political talk."

Anne Martin ran again for the US Senate in 1920 and won more votes, but was again unsuccessful. She left Nevada disillusioned, perhaps feeling that her political losses meant that she had failed in her greater goal. After moving to California, she continued to write articles for newspapers and magazines, and she also contributed to encyclopedias. She received an honorary doctorate of laws degree from the University of Nevada in 1945. It must have seemed like a long time since she had founded the university's History Department as a bright young scholar.

Anne Martin died on April 15, 1951, at the age of 75 in Carmel, California, far from the spotlight of the struggle for equal rights. But it's funny how history works. With the passage of time, the names of her 1918 opponents, Charles Henderson and E. E. Roberts, have largely faded from the history books. Nevadans would be forgiven for not remembering the names of the state's governors in the early 1900s.

But more than a century after she chose the longer, harder road to equal voting rights in the Silver State, it's Anne Martin's name that is well remembered—and should be celebrated.

As historian Anne Bail Howard observes, "Whatever her intentions, her delusions, her mistakes, she made two sincere and stubborn efforts to rally women around a woman candidate; she dared and she gave all her energies to a decade of campaigns, including state suffrage and the federal amendment, two hardy pursuits of the Senate."

Sadie Hurst Breaks Through

Unlike Anne Martin, who reached for the moon in deciding to run for the US Senate, there was another woman running for political office in 1918 in Nevada. Her name was Sadie Hurst. (Edna Baker of Sparks was also elected to the University Board of Regents.) Sadie aimed closer to home by campaigning for a seat in the Assembly.

As a Washoe County suffragist, Sadie was a registered Republican and was active in Reno women's clubs, which promoted discussions of politics and current events, and was a leader in the Washoe County Equal Franchise Society which supported women's voting rights.

Unlike Anne, who was often criticized by the press for being too outspoken, Sadie received the endorsement of the Reno's *Nevada State Journal*.

In the November 1918 endorsement , the newspaper noted that Sadie "has taken an active part in public matters" as a leader of women's clubs in Reno. It is believed to have substantially contributed to her victory.

Mrs. Sadie D. Hurst

Republican Candidate

for the

ASSEMBLY

Solicits the support of the voters
of Washoe County who believe in
state and national prohibition.

**ENDORSED BY THE CLUB
WOMEN OF RENO**

**NOT A MEMBER OF THE
WOMAN'S PARTY**

Sadie Hurst's campaign for the state Assembly was spread through various ways, like this newspaper clipping from 1918.

It also helped that the national attitude toward equal voting rights was changing. President Woodrow Wilson had been slow to actively accept suffrage for women, but the cause was greatly helped in 1918 after he announced his support.

When Nevada women won the right to vote in state elections, they were generally excited to vote for Sadie. She became the first woman elected to the state legislature. Although she served just a single two-year term in the Assembly, she did so at a historic moment. When she was seated in the Assembly in January for the 1919 legislative session, she was sometimes called "Assembly Woman" and sometimes referred to as "Gentle Lady."

Sadie kept busy by introducing eight pieces of legislation. Sadie was successful in presenting a bill that increased the age of consent to marry for girls from sixteen to eighteen years of age. It was a shining moment in her brief legislative career. She made her mark and in doing so helped redefine what was possible for women in Nevada politics.

44

Sadie was a progressive, a person who believed in political action to improve the ills and inequality of society, at a time when Reno was known as a wild town filled with saloons and illegal gambling dens. She also advocated for prohibition as a person who was opposed to the consumption of alcoholic beverages. She believed drinking liquor had a harmful effect on the morals of society at a time when the nation publicly debated the issue. In 1919, Congress passed the Volstead Act, which attempted to carry out the Eighteenth Amendment's prohibition of alcohol. The amendment and law were unpopular and ineffective in preventing Americans from drinking alcohol. The Eighteenth Amendment lasted until 1933, when it was repealed with the ratification of the Twenty-first Amendment.

On January 23, 1919, at the legislature, Sadie introduced the resolution to amend the US Constitution and give women the right to vote in all elections. In the summer of 1919, the Congress moved to pass the Nineteenth Amendment that would guarantee women the right to vote—if the legislatures of three-fourths of the states voted to approve the change to the Constitution.

In a special session of the legislature the following February, Sadie was given the honor of presiding over the full Assembly during the passage of the resolution. On February 7, 1920, the resolution passed on a 25-1 vote and added Nevada to the growing number of states to ratify the Nineteenth Amendment.

Constitutionally Speaking

Learning about the United States Constitution can be confusing, so let's start at the beginning. What is a constitution, anyway?

⇨A **constitution** is a set of basic principles and rights guaranteed by a government for its people. Signed on September 17, 1787, the United States Constitution is the oldest document of its kind in use in the world.

⇨An **amendment** means to make a change or add to something in an effort to improve it. Just two years after the Constitution was first signed, on September 25, 1789, twelve amendments were adopted by Congress and sent to the states for final approval in a process called **ratification**. Ten of the twelve amendments were ratified, and today they are commonly known as the Bill of Rights.

⇨In the United States, amendments to the Constitution are made by the proposed change— voting rights for women, for example—winning votes from two-thirds of the House of Representatives and Senate. The proposed constitutional amendment then proceeds to the states for final ratification. If two-thirds of the states' legislatures vote to ratify the amendment, it then becomes part of the Constitution.

⇨It's important to remember that the Constitution isn't some dusty old piece of parchment. It has been amended a number of times over the years and has grown and changed along with the nation.

Governor Emmet Boyle proclaimed, "While no certainty exists that the favorable action of Nevada will in 1920 assure to the women of the United States the same voting privileges which our own women enjoy by virtue of our state law, it does appear certain that without our favorable action the cause of national suffrage may be delayed for such a time as to withhold the right to vote in a presidential election from millions of the women of America. Under the circumstances it has appeared to me that Nevada may well at this time live up to her chivalrous traditions."

One state legislature after another voted to ratify the amendment. When Tennessee's legislature voted in favor of ratification on August 18, 1920, the Nineteenth Amendment was adopted. The ratification was certified August 26, 1920. American women at last had the right to vote in federal elections.

But in Nevada, equal representation at the legislature and elsewhere in public office would come slowly.

Back on the Road to Equality

Sadie Hurst's groundbreaking election to the Nevada Legislature opened the door for women in politics in the state. Progress was slow. Just forty-two women followed her lead into the legislature over the next 65 years. Gains were made in other offices, most commonly on school boards, but it wasn't until 1966 that Las Vegas Democrat Helen Herr became the first woman elected to the state Senate. Helen, who had served previous terms in the Assembly, remained in the Senate for a decade. Among her many goals were improving the state's mental health system and ensuring equal pay for equal work for women.

When Nevada's growing population qualified it for a second seat in Congress, in 1982 Republican Barbara Vucanovich became the first woman elected to the House of Representatives. She served seven two-year terms and retired in 1996. Her daughter Patricia Cafferata was also a political groundbreaker.

In 1982 she became the first woman in Nevada history to be elected to a constitutional office when she won the statewide race for state treasurer. She later ran unsuccessfully for governor.

Nevada native Frankie Sue Del Papa, a Democrat, spent much of her life breaking gender barriers, initially by becoming the first woman elected student body president at the University of Nevada. In 1986, Del Papa became the first woman elected as Nevada's Secretary of State. After one term, in 1990 she set another first by winning the first of a record three terms as state Attorney General. After leaving office, she remained an outspoken advocate for women in politics.

Lorna Kesterson of Henderson is a name nearly lost to Nevada political history, but in 1985 she became the first woman to be elected mayor in one of the state's larger cities. Far better known is Jan Jones Blackhurst, who in 1991 was elected mayor of Las Vegas and served in the high-profile office throughout the 1990s. Carolyn Goodman in 2011 entered the Mayor's Office in Las Vegas following in her husband Oscar Goodman's footsteps. Up north in Reno, Hillary Schieve in 2014 brought her brand of energy and effort to the mayor's role.

The appearance of women in positions of leadership at the state Legislature was a long time coming. It wasn't until 2007 that Barbara Buckley rose to Assembly Speaker, and not until 2019 that Nicole Cannizaro was named Senate Majority Leader.

The expansion of equal representation remains a work in progress in Nevada. As of 2020, no woman had yet been elected Governor. Democrat Dina Titus came closest in 2006, losing a spirited race to Jim Gibbons. Undaunted, she went on to serve multiple terms in Congress.

Nevada women did, however, break through to the position of lieutenant governor, where Republican Sue Wagner was elected in 1990. In the legislature, Wagner served with distinction, leading special studies on reforming the state prison system and foster care program. She sponsored successful bills affecting families, women, children, and persons with disabilities, among many.

Republican Lorraine Hunt served two terms as lieutenant governor after winning the election in 1998. In 2018, former senior deputy attorney general Kate Marshall was elected lieutenant governor. Marshall, a Democrat, had previously served two terms as Nevada's treasurer and championed the state's college savings plan.

Women of color and Native American women struggled to climb through Nevada's political ranks a century after the passage of the Nineteenth Amendment. Democrat Bernice Mathews served fifteen years in the state Senate from Washoe County as the first Black woman elected to the legislature.

Bernice's personal story was a reminder of how far a woman of color could progress despite life's

US Senator Jacky Rosen joins former Nevada Senator Bernice Mathews to donate books to the Bernice Mathews Elementary School in Reno.

obstacles. Born in Jackson, Mississippi, in an era of severe racial segregation, Bernice spent years improving her education. As her legislative colleague Mo Denis reflected at the time of her induction into the Nevada Senate Hall of Fame, "Former Senator Mathews' life is a testimony to the importance and power of education. . . . As a student, growing up in the segregated South, she understood what it was to be denied equal opportunities to study."

And when those opportunities came, Bernice took advantage of them, earning a nursing certificate and degrees from the University of Nevada.

Native Americans, meanwhile, continue to struggle to be heard in the halls of the legislature. It wasn't until the 2019 session of the legislature that the first woman of Native American heritage was elected. Democrat Shea Backus, a Nevada native and enrolled member of the Cherokee Nation, entered the Assembly as an attorney with training in Native American legal issues.

US Senator Catherine Cortez Masto speaks in the Senate chamber.

It was also in the 2019 session of the Nevada Legislature that something truly monumental happened. For the first time in American history, and almost 100 years after the ratification of the Nineteenth Amendment giving women the right to vote, a state legislature was led by a female majority.

And it happened in Nevada.

In the new century Nevada's congressional delegation better reflected the state's diversity on the Democratic side of the aisle with Titus, Shelley Berkley, Susie Lee, Jacky Rosen, and African American Steven Horsford serving multiple terms in the House. Rosen in

2018 was elected to the Senate.

Perhaps the biggest breakthrough for women and people of color was the 2016 election of former Nevada Attorney General Catherine Cortez Masto to the United States Senate. In doing so, she became the first woman elected to the Senate in Nevada history, and the first Latina elected to that position in American history.

So many years after a young woman from Empire City wondered in her diary whether she would ever accomplish anything, the answer sings on the fair winds of change throughout the Silver State.

Glossary

Congress: The US Congress is a legislative body that consists of 100 senators, two from each state, and 435 members of the House of Representatives, whose numbers are divided based on a state's population.

disenfranchise: to deprive someone of a right or privilege, such as voting rights.

Nevada Legislature: a lawmaking body consisting of the Senate and the Assembly.

Nineteenth Amendment: Once ratified on August 18, 1920, this amendment to the US Constitution gave all female American citizens at least 21 years old the right to vote in all elections.

progressive: a political philosophy in support of social reform.

Prohibition: legal prevention of the sale and manufacture of alcoholic beverages made into law by the 18th Amendment.

ratify, ratification: a formal, official confirmation of something, usually by a vote.

Silent Sentinels: A group of women in favor of women's suffrage that protested in front of the White House without saying a word.

suffrage: the right to vote in political elections.

Cast of Characters

Anne Martin: As a suffragist and pacifist, Anne was an outspoken advocate for women's rights.

Bird Wilson: Vice president of the Equal Franchise Society and the seventh licensed female attorney in Nevada, Bird wrote a pamphlet titled *Woman Under Nevada Laws*.

Curtis Hillyer: A member of the Nevada Assembly who, in 1869, spoke up on behalf of women's suffrage.

Elizabeth Cady Stanton: A major figure in the American suffrage movement, Elizabeth was born in New York and advocated both the Nineteenth and the Thirteenth Amendments.

Emma Adams: Wife of former Nevada governor Jewett Adams, she served as president of the Nevada Association of Women Opposed to Equal Suffrage.

Emmet Boyle: The thirteenth governor of Nevada who took office in 1915.

Felice Cohn: Working to lobby government change from inside, Felice was one of the first women admitted to practice law before the US Supreme Court.

Francis Newlands: A politician from Nevada who served in the US House of Representatives and Senate.

Susan B. Anthony: A suffrage pioneer from Massachusetts who founded the National Woman Suffrage Association. Her portrait was chosen to be on the one-dollar coin in 1979, making her the first women to be so honored.

Selected Bibliography and Further Reading

Bennett, Dana Rae. "'Undismayed by Any Mere Man:' Women Lawmakers and Tax Policy in Nevada, 1919–1956." Dissertation, 2019. Arizona State University.

Gault, James. *Writings of James Gault*. Sparks, NV: Sparks Tribune Printers, 1914.

Her Hat Was in the Ring! website and database: http://www. herhatwasinthering.org/biography.php?id=4870

Howard, Anne Bail. *The Long Campaign: A Biography of Anne Martin*. Reno: University of Nevada Press, 1985.

Hutcheson, Austin E., Editor. "The Story of the Nevada Equal Suffrage Campaign: Memoirs of Anne Martin." Reno, NV: University of Nevada Bulletin Vol. XLIII: No. 7 (August 1948)

Neuman, Johanna. *And Yet they Persisted: How American Women Won the Right to Vote*. Hoboken, NJ: Wiley Blackwell, 2020.

Nevada Women's History Project. https://www.nevadawomen.org

Anne Martin: The March for Suffrage
Questions for Discussion

1. Why was it important for women to have the right to vote?
2. In addition to voting rights, what other issues were women concerned with in Nevada?
3. What powerful business leader and political influencer was opposed to equal voting rights in Nevada?
4. How did Nevada compare to other states in the West when it came to the issue of equal suffrage?
5. Did some men also support equal voting rights for women? Name one, and discuss.
6. Equal suffrage for women took many years to become law. Why was the struggle worth it?
7. Did women win elected office often in the first years after suffrage was gained?
8. What happened to the Nevada Legislature and other elected offices after the passage of the Nineteenth Amendment?
9. What did Helen Herr accomplish, and why was it important?
10. What did Nevada women lawmakers accomplish, and why is it important?

About the Author

Native Nevadan John L. Smith is a longtime journalist and the author of more than a dozen books including *Saints, Sinners, and Sovereign Citizens: The Endless War Over the West's Public Lands*. He has won many state, regional, and national awards for his writing and was inducted into the Nevada Press Association Newspaper Hall of Fame in 2016, the same year that saw him honored with the James Foley/Medill  Medal for Courage in Journalism, the Society of Professional Journalists Ethics Award, and the Ancil Payne Award for Ethics in Journalism from the University of Oregon. He freelances for a variety of publications, including *The Nevada Independent*. The father of a grown daughter, Amelia, he is married to the writer Sally Denton and makes his home in Boulder City, Nevada.

Don't miss a single adventure!

Read all the books in the Fields of Silver and Gold series.

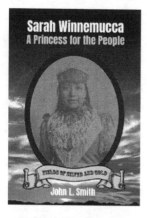

#1 **Sarah Winnemucca:**
A Princess for the People

#2 **Snowshoe Thompson:**
Sierra Mailman

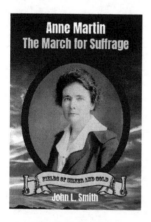

#3 **Anne Martin:**
The March for Suffrage

#4 **Ben Palmer:**
Black Pioneers on the Frontier

Coming Fall 2021:

#5 and #6 - *Details coming soon to keystonecanyon.com*